# INTERMISSION

*Spiritual Refreshment for the Drama Ministry Team*

# INTERMISSION

## Spiritual Refreshment for the Drama Ministry Team

### A Collection of Twelve Teaching Devotionals

BY

## JEFFREY D. FRAME

illenas PUBLISHING COMPANY

KANSAS CITY, MO 64141

# Dedication

To Kim, my wife and best friend,
and our loving daughters, Jillian and Hilary

# Contents

# Acknowledgments

A special thank you to:

Kim, who keeps me caffeinated, sane, and sanguine all at the same time

Jillian and Hilary, the joy at both ends of my rainbow

Mom and Dad, who have forged my life with God's grace and love

Ronda and Carl Winderl, my lifelong friends and the generous mentors of my formative days at college and beyond

Kim Messer and Stacey Schnarr, who maintain a perfect 4.0 in publishing and patience!

Dean Blevins, for your iron-sharpening friendship and faithful encouragement

# Introduction

## *The Word Enacted*

One has only to glance from the East Coast to the West to see the wide variety of church laity in our country who are involved in drama ministry. Regardless of denomination, geographical location, age-group, or cultural differences, the unique challenges facing drama ministry teams seem to be similar almost everywhere.

We seem to share common questions about how to inspire and challenge the different groups represented within our churches. We wonder how we can gain the confidence of our congregations and how we can develop mutual support between our drama ministry team and our pastoral leadership. We yearn for tight scripts and compelling characters that speak intimately to our hearts. We want to know more about theatre and how our God-given dramatic talents might be given back to glorify our Heavenly Father.

However, these questions are not easy ones to answer. The love-hate relationship between theatre and the church goes nearly as far back as the history of the church itself, and our entertainment-saturated, media-frenzied American culture has tended to intensify that relationship throughout the 20th century. Neal Gabler suggests in his book *Life: The Movie* that our society has evolved into one that must be entertained before it can be engaged. Laser light shows in the sanctuary and cappuccino carts in the foyer are rapidly becoming the norm, rather than the exception, in the megachurch movement.

Nevertheless, we remember, too, that drama can be a powerful ministerial tool, if used responsibly. We do not desire the "applause of men," but the genuine, Spirit-called sharing of the gospel of Christ through the power of the Word enacted. We recognize that as the message is transformed from the page onto the stage, we experience something immediate and wonderfully incarnational that refocuses our minds and hearts more keenly on the Word Incarnate. We steadfastly believe that our sovereign Creator can use us through the performing arts of drama, music, and dance to build His kingdom.

Although the questions and needs of drama ministry are many, they often easily divide into two distinct categories: those that deal directly with our ministry to others and those that focus on the group dynamics and spiritual growth within the drama ministry team itself. And because the questions and needs of drama ministry are unique, they are perhaps best satisfied with unique responses.

One of those responses takes the form of this devotional book—a collection of devotional discussions unlike others in that it speaks to the specific questions, needs, and challenges faced by most drama ministry teams today. *Each discussion invites us to consider carefully how we can minister with greater impact through drama and how we can encourage each other in the process.* In fact, constructing meaningful devotional time together is an essential part of every healthy drama ministry team's routine and cannot be ignored, regardless of how fast you are going or how little time your group has to rehearse. Process *must* be as important as product in drama ministry.

The collection is unique also because each discussion is really a "teaching devotional." In other words, the discussions serve as teaching tools since each one explains an important theatrical idea or concept as well. *The devotionals do not attempt to teach theatrical skills per se, but rather focus on basic dramatic knowledge important to both beginning and experienced drama ministry teams.*

## Passion and Compassion in Drama Ministry

Each of us tends to be either task-oriented or maintenance-oriented. Task-oriented people focus on getting a job done. They are concerned that a goal be set and accomplished and seek rather single-mindedly to hurdle all obstacles in order to get there. On the other hand, maintenance-oriented folks are more interested in taking care of the people they meet along the way. If they are part of a group, they are usually the first to make sure that the members of the group are well cared for. They are more sensitive and try to nurture positive relationships. Ask many people, and they will hastily say that most men tend to be task-oriented creatures and that most women are of a maintenance-oriented nature.

Similarly, a theatre director or drama ministry leader can lean more in one of these directions than another. If a director is more task-oriented, he or she may be more concerned about what the final production will look like. "Product" is the end-all of their labors, and all they do is designed to help them get to that point effectively. In contrast, directors who are maintenance-oriented push for "process." They are more excited about the learning and ministry that is taking place in rehearsals and during internal group work than they are about presenting work for an audience. For them, the means becomes the end, and an audience is not required for success.

Ideally, a good director will combine both approaches. But such a feat of juggling is not an easy one to sustain for long periods of time. How does one exude a passion (task-orientation) for ministry through drama while at the same time express a compassion (maintenance-orientation) for the people with whom we minister (i.e., our own drama ministry team)?

In the New Testament, the use of the Greek words *poiema* ("dedicated workmanship") and *koinonia* ("fellowship") suggest that this delicate balance is important to successful drama ministry development. Perhaps one of the most meaningful aspects of this devotional book is that its structure and language deliberately attempt to foster such a balance.

## Suggestions for Using the Devotionals

The following 12 devotionals alternate intermittently between topics that address the needs within a drama ministry team *(koinonia)* and the needs that are represented externally in the team-congregation relationship *(poiema)*. A "K" near the title indicates *koinonia* or a maintenance-based devotional, while a "P" denotes *poiema* or a task-based devotional.

In scriptwriting and in scene analysis, subtext is considered to be the inner thought or feeling of a character, regardless of outward dialogue. Subtext is not simply reading the lines; it is reading between and perhaps even beyond the lines (an area that is explored later in a devotional). Television variety shows and sitcoms especially have capitalized on the delightful comic incongruities that can occur between what is said and what is actually thought at the same time.

Although the devotionals here obviously do not aim for the same effect, they do use text and subtext to clarify pertinent connections between the scripture passage offered (from the *New Revised Standard Version*) and our own involvement in drama ministry. With the scripture excerpt at the beginning serving as our text, or focal point of the study, the body of the devotional becomes our subtext—our search for at least some of what lies tucked away for us within the text. Both the opening epigram and the scriptural text are often alluded to throughout the subtext of the devotional.

While reflecting on the text and subtext, perhaps the most transforming aspect of each devotional study becomes the drama ministry team's responses to the context sections that divide the larger subtext into smaller, more palatable discussions. The questions offered may be used either for reflection or for discussion, or both, depending on the needs of your group. *Because each devotional is rather substantive and because your rehearsal time is precious, you will probably want to extend each devotional over the course of three to four weeks.* Possible prayer needs for the team, based on the devotional topic, are also suggested directly after each study.

The book may be used by drama ministry teams at almost any level of development and in a number of ways. Of course, rehearsal time is always the challenge, and knowing how to best use one's devotional time together is an important launching point. One effective approach to healthy stewardship of rehearsal/devotional time is for everyone in the team to read the same preselected devotional (or portion of a devotional) ahead of time at home and to be prepared to discuss the contextual questions and scripture at rehearsal.

This approach gives team members an opportunity to reflect on the questions before meeting to discuss them. If a group does have the rare luxury of extra time, then having someone read the full devotional at the meeting might be an excellent way of digging more deeply for insights into the material. How you choose to divide the reading will depend partly on the frequency and length of your meetings. A sample rehearsal/devotional time line for a simple two-hour rehearsal might look something like this:

- First 5 minutes: Begin with a song or improvisational activity to get the juices flowing and to produce a creative atmosphere
- Next 45 minutes: Jump right into serious work on the play or musical, especially scenes requiring a lot of concentration and/or energy.
- Break for 5 minutes
- Return for a 15-minute devotional
- 5 minutes of group prayer
- Next 35 minutes: Continue into serious rehearsal work in scenes that are easier than the first set
- End the last 10 minutes with notes and housekeeping items

This kind of structure (or a similar variation) helps to keep casts from getting bored with either your devotional time or your rehearsal proper.

Once while traveling home from a Work and Witnes trip to Arizona, I stood on the edge of the Grand Canyon and watched an eagle slowly make its way up, up from the canyon floor all the way to the top. What was so impressive was that the bird never beat its wings. Instead, it simply spread its wings and, in a large spiral, rode the warm air coming up from the summer currents until it finally glided to the top. Wow!

Those currents reminded me of what devotional time with God does for our rehearsals. We can beat our wings until our feathers fall out and still be no higher than the first ledge of the canyon. But when we make the time to allow God to carry us up, up to new heights, our faith grows and He really takes us places we never knew we could go! Perhaps that's all to say, devotional time in rehearsal is not as much a matter of *finding time* as it is a matter of correctly *prioritizing time*.

Finally, several supplemental lists of information follow the collection of devotionals to assist your team with further discussion and exploration. First, you will find an optional list of suggested additional scripture readings for each devotional—all of which are related to each opening devotional text and are appropriate for extended study. There is also a brief list of drama resources dealing with topics related to the one presented in each devotional discussion. Resources include both Lillenas publications and other prominent titles in the field. For clarification of key terms and people introduced in some of the discussions, a glossary has been provided. The last list is an appendix of improvisation exercises designed to support each devotional topic—directly or indirectly—with a lively, yet meaningful activity.

## *We Interrupt This Mission*

We all know how valuable an intermission at a play performance can be. They throw a cliffhanger at us, followed by a short break between acts so we can stretch, get the circulation flowing again, discuss the scenes we've just watched, get a drink of water, and so on.

Would we fully appreciate, then, what an "intermission" within our own drama ministry activities might do for us? Could we come to understand what it really means to "interrupt our mission" briefly between "acts" so we can take time to stretch our minds, to experience the Holy Spirit circulating in and through us, to share our faith more intimately with each other, and to receive the refreshing Living Water?

The discussions to follow are an open invitation to do just that. As we do, may we individually and collectively take stock of our walk with Christ and make necessary time for the spiritual refreshment and blessings God intends for us.

# "What's My Motivation?"

### K

*"Spiritual maturity begins when we realize*
*that we are God's guests in this world."*
—C. Willard Fetter

## Text:

"All one's ways may be pure in one's own eyes, but the LORD weighs the spirit. Commit your work to the LORD, and your plans will be established" (Prov. 16:2-3).

## Subtext:

You are well into your third hour of rehearsal, and the natives are getting restless. You are as eager as your director is about making the production a success, both spiritually and artistically, but even you are getting tired. Your director changes your blocking yet again, instructing you to cross down right to the mantel of the fireplace, this time in the middle of your most important speech. And as you do, the question finally, slowly breaks itself free from your innermost thoughts, floating to the surface of your impatience until at last it sheepishly lands on your lips: "But what's my motivation?"

The great director and acting coach Konstantin Stanislavsky first introduced it to actors. Over the past century, serious Method actors have relied on it time and again. Today, their comic counterparts make sport of it both on television and in film.... That famous, if not exhausted question "What's my motivation?" is one that has been asked by actors in earnest and in jest at more rehearsals than perhaps any other question in the recent history of theatre. But in spite of the abuse it suffers regularly, the question still packs some powerful concepts that are vital to the actor and, in a much more compelling way, to the serious drama ministry team.

Unsuccessful drama ministry efforts tend to flounder and fail more from subtle misguidance or a lack of direction than from any other single cause. Drama ministry leadership and participants often not only forget to consider the "why?" about drama ministry but also what acting teacher Robert Cohen might call the "what for?" It's not enough for a group to know only what drives or "motivates" its drama ministry at church. What does our group intend to accomplish through that ministry? Are these *our* intentions or *God's*? How easy it can be to get sidetracked, mistaking our goals for God's perfect design in the process!

## Context (Questions for Reflection or Discussion):

*Why use drama as a form of ministry in our church at all? Aren't other ministries such as Sunday School, music, prayer, and preaching sufficient? Why or why not? When we say that drama has a uniquely incarnational power in ministry, what do we mean?*

Some of the newest PCs now allow you to pick the "voice" you will hear when your operating system sends you an error message. Simply scroll through the voices until you find one that works for you! We live in a culture that expects us to listen to and to tolerate many different voices and then to find our own voice—a voice that we can conveniently adopt for ourselves. This postmodern phenomenon of many different, conflicting voices (known as *heterōglossia*) creates a clamoring competition for our allegiances. Banner ads on the Internet vie for our attention by screaming at our eyes, television commercials seductively suggest that we can "have it our way," and political-cultural-spiritual pluralism has never been more prevalent. True, for the theatre practitioner there lies a certain appeal and even some validity in finding one's own creative, artistic voice. But when it comes time to profess Christ and to implement a drama ministry mission statement, there can be only one Voice speaking, and we desperately need to be listening to Him.

## Context (Questions for Reflection or Discussion):

*Why is each of us involved in drama ministry? What do we each expect to receive from it? What are we willing to sacrifice in order to achieve excellence both in ministry and in art as we seek to glorify God? How can God use us on-stage and off?*

When Stanislavsky gave us motivation as a technique for acting, he meant that we should justify within ourselves the reason for our own character's attitudes and behaviors. Likewise, it would be easy for each of us to justify internally our own reasons for choosing to minister through drama. Some would claim that drama significantly improves worship on Sunday morning. Others might cite Jesus' frequent use of teaching through metaphors and parables as a way to connect with (or, at times, confuse) the masses. Still others might see the stage as one more opportunity for self-expression or as a soapbox for imposing their own opinions (unfortunately, but quite humanly, there is a little brazen exhibitionism in all of us who are involved with theatre!).

As we begin then to self-examine the purpose of our drama ministry at our church, we should not be asking "What is *our motivation?*" but rather "What, Father, are *Your intended outcomes and expectations?*" At the risk of oversimplifying the obvious, we must always address in the most sincere, most prayerful way whether the drama ministry we share together has become *our* ministry instead of *His* ministry. Both Prov. 16:2-3 and the familiar Heb. 12:1-2 effectively remind us that just about the time everything seems to be working the way we think it should, it's actually time for God to check our motives. Lest we become blinded by the self-serving brightness of the proverbial limelight, it is *He* who ultimately weighs our individual spirits. We must *truly* acknowledge His sovereignty over all that we are, in performance and in the wings. Only then can we begin to discover (in spite of ourselves) the rich blessings and unimaginable miracles that will unfold through the incarnational power of drama and into the lives of those with whom we bear witness to God's love and grace.

## Context (Questions for Reflection or Discussion):

*What does it really mean to be a selfless actor, director, or designer in Christ? If theatre is such a collaborative art, why can't we work together better? Do we keep our eyes on Christ, or on someone else who has what we think we want?*

## Suggestions for Prayer:

- Discernment of God's true intention and vision for our ministry
- Formation of Christlike unity and purpose within our drama team
- Honest self-examination of our own reasons for participating

# Fast-Food Drama Ministry

---
## P
---

"I'm addicted to placebos. I'd quit, but it wouldn't really matter."
—Stephen Wright, comedian

## Text:

"You are the salt of the earth; but if salt has lost its taste, how can its saltiness be restored? It is no longer good for anything, but is thrown out and trampled under foot. You are the light of the world. A city built on a hill cannot be hid" (Matt. 5:13-14).

## Subtext:

In the movie *What About Bob?* actor Richard Dreyfuss plays a frustrated psychiatrist who escapes with his family to their remote summer home for vacation. While there, he is plagued by his hilariously intrusive, deceptively intelligent patient Bob (Bill Murray), all to the innocent delight of his wife and children. One of the funniest moments in the movie results when the disrupted family must huddle together to work through their differences using their family puppets, each one bearing an uncanny resemblance to the respective family member who wears it. The discussion that follows is designed to permit each person the freedom to express his or her own "true" feelings without resorting to any direct confrontation.

Of course, the film's absurd parody of this popular counseling technique using puppets reveals, in fact, that no real dialogue is taking place at all. A watered-down substitute for meaningful dialogue has amounted to little more than an exercise in emptiness and miscommunication.

So what has this got to do with drama ministry? Suppose our pastor has asked us to put a sketch together addressing some choices and consequences of alcohol abuse within a scriptural context. Confidently, we agree to give it a go and succeed in whipping up a safe scenario that quickly introduces the problem, intensifies the conflict, and delivers a payoff verse that answers every question raised. All of it is neatly packaged into a tidy three-minute sermon starter. Is there anything wrong with this picture?

Let's take a peek. Can the physiological disease of alcoholism really be approached, carefully examined, and assessed spiritually all in the course of three minutes? And although drama does indeed provide through role-play a way to test choices and consequences in a low-risk environment, can the entire issue of alcohol abuse be simply and "safely" tackled in a worship setting?

Realistically, no, on both counts. The pastor has given us a formidable task, one that is probably better suited for an occasion outside of worship. Yet we are committed to our pastor's request and to his or her underlying vision for worship ministry; so we press on. Instead of the safe scenario, however (which would most likely result in a shallow dialogue similar to the one manufactured by the puppet family), we choose to focus on real lives at stake and on a particular cause of alcoholism. We resist the temptation to oversimplify the characters and their circumstances. Moreover, we decide to produce more questions than answers—a meaningful, realistic approach—and to allow our pastor, rightfully and carefully, to provide God's responses in the sermon to follow.

## Context (Questions for Reflection or Discussion):

*How does our pastoral staff support the drama ministry team? How does the drama ministry team support our pastor(s)? Is our senior pastor open to dialogue sermons, heavy-duty (challenging, rather than inspiring) worship sketches, and longer dramatic works that pack a punch (and not a lunch!)?*

Rather than spoon-feeding us with easy answers or with cheap substitutes for difficult choices, good drama should raise tough questions. Effective drama ministry calls us to higher levels of thinking and understanding and eventually into a closer, covenant relationship with the One who does meet all of our needs. Unfortunately, however, we too often prepare theatre of spiritual significance as a dessert dish and forget to include the meat-and-potatoes nourishment that defines compelling theatre and life-changing ministry. Whether we go for the hard-hitting, issue-oriented drama or for the lighter humor to help "the medicine go down," we are always at risk of becoming addicted to spiritual placebos. How could this happen? It's easy: we simply avoid what we *really* need to talk about in our spiritual lives, and replace it with the things that make us feel good all the time, the things that make us *feel* like we are getting what we need.

When cyberdegrees pose as college educations, when E-mail masquerades as authentic interpersonal communication, and when the extra-value meal from our favorite burger drive-thru substitutes for a healthy, home-cooked meal, it's no wonder we so easily subscribe to watered-down spirituality and fast-food worship services. Sound bites, one-stop shopping, and speed dialing. Our society boasts a fast-food mind-set that permeates even our most diligent drama ministry efforts. Fast-food, feel-good drama ministry equals immediate gratification, no seasoning required. Just add water. Yuck!

How then can we possibly slow down again? How do we again "accept no substitutes" for meaningful drama experiences in our churches? How do we weed out the trite clichés and the quick fixes in our performances so that our drama ministry team remains fresh and vital to the ministry opportunities around us? How can our "saltiness" be restored if we have lost our taste?

## Context (Questions for Reflection or Discussion):

*Nonna Childress Dalan (founding member of the Christians in Theatre Arts organization) has suggested that "holy shoddy is still shoddy." How can we keep our drama ministry (and our puppet ministry, for that matter) from getting a bad rap because of what Dalan calls holy shoddiness? Are we sloppy with our work? Do we do our homework in preparation for a sketch or production? Are we dedicated to giving our best effort in reverence to our Creator?*

Let us remember to take time with God's message, take time with the dramatic material, take time with each other. Slowly. Let us not throw skits and scenery together haphazardly. Let us not hurry through our group prayers before service. Let us not inadvertently cheapen our gifts from God. Let us discern God's will from our spiritual (and theatrical) sugar pills. Let us keep praying, reading Scripture, sharing accountability with one another, and exercising our faith in and obedience to Christ. Let us keep on keeping on! Let us not be afraid to dig carefully, prayerfully— to dig a little deeper and to reach the very depths of our questioning, so that God might lift us up in His grace and guidance and remind us that our loving Father was, is, and will remain the great I AM.

## Context (Questions for Reflection or Discussion):

*Is our congregation ready for the medium and the message that theatre has to offer them, or do we need to approach them gradually, using "baby steps" (an-other* What About Bob? *bit)?*

## Suggestions for Prayer:

- Our pastoral staff and lay leaders
- Guidance over future sketch and play selection
- Our Christlike sensitivity and openness to consider material that will raise questions that challenge and strengthen our faith

# Prima Donna 101

---
K
---

"Let me say something about ethics in the theatre. [One] reason for the collapse of well-intentioned venture after venture is sloth and egomania. We must accept the fact that the theatre is a communal adventure. Unlike the soloist, we can't perform alone in the theatre.... The better the play, the more we need an ensemble venture. We must recognize that we need each other's strengths, and the more we need each other's professional comradeship, the better the chance we have of making theatre. We must serve the play by serving each other; an ego-maniacal 'star' attitude is only self-serving and hurts everyone....

"We must aim for character in the moral and ethical sense of the word, compounded of the virtues of mutual respect, courtesy, kindness, generosity, trust, attention to the others, seriousness, loyalty, as well as those necessary attributes of diligence and dedication."

—Uta Hagen, *Respect for Acting*

## Text:

"And all of you must clothe yourselves with humility in your dealings with one another, for 'God opposes the proud, but gives grace to the humble.' Humble yourselves therefore under the mighty hand of God, so that he may exalt you in due time" (1 Pet. 5:5-6).

## Subtext:

"Hey, wait a minute! What's Uta up to? Hagen's hoggin' the stage here. Stealing my thunder. She's in my limelight. I've been upstaged by Uta." Only problem is, she's right. And after a whopper quote like hers, what's left to say?

First of all, let's back up a bit. What does it mean to be in someone's limelight, anyway? After candles and before electricity, there was considerable experimentation in stage technology with ways to better illuminate the stage. One discovery quickly made by 19th-century theatre technicians was the relative brightness of the light created by burning lime in front of a reflective dish. Not long after this discovery, limelight was used for any given moment onstage when particular actions or characters needed to be given more focus or extra attention from the audience. The light was much brighter in those instances, giving immediate emphasis to whatever was lit. It didn't take long for this new method of emphasizing stage action through lighting to be abused by the star system that was already in place.

Now let's back up even farther. During the Italian Renaissance when proscenium "picture frame" stages became popular for creating theatrical illusion, many of the designers and painters became preoccupied with the appearance of perspective onstage. In addition to the perspective painting that was used on nearly every one of their backdrops for productions, one of the earliest developments of this perspective approach was the raked stage. A stage that is raked is simply one that gradually slopes up at a gentle angle from the front of the stage to the back. As a result, actors would actually move upward as they walked away from the audience onstage.

From the raked stage of the Italian Renaissance, we have received the directorial terms *upstage* and *downstage*. So whenever an actor was upstage of other actors in a scene, the others were forced to turn their backs to the audience to look at the actor who was physically farther upstage. That actor received all the focus from everyone, and voilá! …*upstaging* was born!

## Context (Questions for Reflection or Discussion):

*When have we ever "stolen" the limelight from someone else onstage? off-stage? What are some ways we tend to upstage each other in ordinary life situations? How can we better learn to "share" the stage with our acting partners?*

OK, enough theatre history. What's this got to do with Uta's ethics and prima donnas (Italian for "first lady" and first used to denote the leading female singer of an opera company)? It would seem that nearly every person who claims to have been bitten by the acting bug has at some point had the urge to upstage others. Each has felt at least a temporary "love for lime." Upstaging and limelight have relatively innocent beginnings. Yet, our selfish pride has repeatedly shoved itself in the way. For extroverts, it is natural to want to be the center of attention. And for talented performers, there may even be a sense of rightfully deserving a shining moment in the spotlight.

Christ's humility is diametrically opposed to the doctrine of the spotlight, however. Throughout human history and God's story as revealed in Scripture, we see again and again God's preference for the obscure and (sometimes painfully) ironic. From Joseph's delivery out of the hands of his own brothers to Moses' delivery out of the hands of his adoptive Egyptian brother, from the secret of Samson's hair to the pebble in David's sling, from the lowly manger to the criminal's crucifixion—God, in His matchless, incomprehensible, unconditional love for us has shown himself to be loving and humble in the presence of His own creation through the person of His Son, Jesus Christ.

## Context (Questions for Reflection or Discussion):

*What are some examples from our own experiences of God dealing with us in an obscure or ironic way? Why does God choose to reveal himself subtly and usually only a little bit at a time?*

How do we—the actors, extroverts, and star personalities in our church or on our drama ministry team—genuinely humble ourselves before God and before one another? Are we so smug as to assume that our talents give us an automatic "in" with Christ? Do we find ourselves scoffing at the singing abilities of others, throwing our noses up at the sound guy, gossiping dangerously about the dramatic shortcomings of the poorly cast leads? Are we called to be presumptuous about how God can or cannot satisfy the needs of others through a worship sketch, dramatic monologue, or seasonal musical that doesn't happen to meet our own personal standards?

In our quest for artistic excellence, it is tempting to slip into what might be coined "spiritual snobbery." While the potential for ministry may indeed be more likely to increase with presentations that are excellent, if not flawless, God does not live in this box. He can use anyone He chooses for His purposes; He does not always need those with superior diction, exuberant stage presence, or visceral acting abilities (as Moses might attest). College administrator and former pastor Dr. Millard Reed has occasionally described sin as the "delusion of self-sovereignty" in that our sin fools us into believing and behaving as if we should govern our own lives and bow down to no one else but the self. In a sense, our sinful pride makes prima donnas of us all at some point along our journey. None of us are worthy of God's gift of redemptive grace. He offers it to us freely anyway. Let us learn to follow Christ's example and to encourage everyone to do his or her very best, knowing that God in His perfection will take care of all the rest!

## Context (Questions for Reflection or Discussion):

*Can we identify someone at our church or on our drama ministry team who has seriously ruffled our feathers because of his or her superior attitude onstage or backstage? How ought we respond to this person according to Scripture? How have we ignored our responsibility to examine ourselves and to check our own attitudes?*

## Suggestions for Prayer:

- Courage to face those among the Body of Believers who have upset or hurt us in the past and to ask for forgiveness for harboring negative, spiritually unhealthy feelings about them over time
- The ability to perceive objectively our own shortcomings in the attitude department and to seek out emotional accountability among those who are spiritual pillars of our church body

# You Don't Bring Me Backdrops Anymore

---
## P
---

"There is no creativity without faith."
—Thornton Wilder

## Text:

"For truly I tell you, if you have faith the size of a mustard seed, you will say to this mountain, 'Move from here to there,' and it will move; and nothing will be impossible for you" (Matt. 17:20).

## Subtext:

When he wrote *Our Town,* the Pulitzer prize-winning novelist and playwright Thornton Wilder demonstrated how powerfully he had been influenced by the theatrical conventions of Asian theatre, which he had studied on numerous occasions during his visits to the East. The particular style of theatre made popular in the U.S. by Wilder and others who had encountered the Noh theatre of Japan came to be referred to as "minimalism."

What these playwrights chose to show the audience onstage in terms of scenery, props, and costuming was intentionally minimal and deliberately devoid of the more spectacular conventions of stage illusion. The end result of this voluntary simplicity in performance is that the audience has been invited to participate more fully through the active engagement of their own imaginations. This is especially true of *Our Town,* in which the scantily clad stage speaks not only to the minimalist style of production but to some of the play's themes about human value and life as well. Of course, Shakespeare and his contemporaries had already made a regular practice of this kind of thing, and even now, minimalism is prevalent on today's stage as evidenced, for instance, in the 1998 *(How I Learned to Drive)* and 1999 *(Wit)* winners of the Pulitzer prize in drama.

Unfortunately, many theatre groups, including most of our drama ministry teams, suffer from low or nonexistent budgets and are forced into rather involuntary simplicity for the staging of most of the scripts produced. Our productions usually cannot compete with the sprawling passion plays of the 2,000-member churches with their angelic zip lines and their all-too-graphic Golgothan blood-lettings. On the other hand, can't little be much when God is in it? Perhaps if we look in the right places, we can find even in our own drama ministry the same beauty that Wilder found—a beauty that is inherently a part of theatrical simplicity.

## Context (Questions for Reflection or Discussion):

*Reflect on some past productions your church or drama ministry team has presented. Which of them best seem to exemplify this kind of theatrical simplicity? Which ones were involuntarily simple, yet seemed to be more compelling or meaningful because of that same simplicity? How can God use minimalism to speak to our audiences?*

We know that theatre is one of the most symbolic forms of artistic expression among the media and performing arts. We need not try to match film in its ultra-realistic depiction of reality on the screen. Instead, we can seek mere suggestion (and the power of it) on the stage, because that is what theatre does best: suggest. We sometimes wish for space and money to build a revolve on our sanctuary platform or to hang a 30'-wide star drop in front of the baptismal. Of course it is entirely possible, if not desirable, to create the world of the play without a backdrop or a single flat. A manger scene can indeed be compelling, memorable, even life-changing without a manger.

However, the conspicuous absence of scenery requires even greater skill on our part in the areas of directing and acting. Like a poet with words on a page, we must be able to communicate a lot of meaning using a minimal amount of plasticity, or stage apparatus. Yes, some plays do have a few basic requirements for scenery that cannot be avoided for either logistical or thematic reasons. However, we cannot underestimate the power of suggestion and the possibilities of beauty in simple but carefully directed/performed presentations. (This is one of the reasons that readers theatre is such an attractive choice for presentation in many drama ministry environments.)

## Context (Questions for Reflection or Discussion):

*Has our church or drama ministry team ever tried readers theatre as a form of ministry? Why or why not? Why might our congregation be more receptive to readers theatre than to other forms of drama ministry?*

There are few things worse in drama ministry efforts than watching a team attempt to mount an enormous production with all the frills and trimmings, and then to see them do it so poorly. Those kinds of well-intentioned but misguided undertakings are partially what stigmatize drama ministry programs in many churches. Instead, we may articulate God's message more profoundly by using the simple, powerful tools of symbol and metaphor through our careful selection and implementation of only a few token props, set pieces, or costume accessories.

We should also learn to trust the collective imagination of our congregational audience more. If we give them some credit for their ability to make meaningful connections, if we allow them to construct their own meanings from the dramatic material with the help of the Holy Spirit, and if we empower them with more sophisticated, artistic sensibilities through the creation of art forms that challenge us in our relationships with Christ to think and feel outside of the box, then we have begun to discover the full potential of drama as a ministry.

The bottom line is our faith in God's creativity and power. We spend so much time trying to spread a theatrical banquet on the table for our guests that we often lose sight of how God can use our dramatic fish and loaves to meet everyone's needs from a simple lunch sack.

Although the circumstances are similar in many ways, Jesus' words to His disciples and the centurion in Matt. 8 are slightly different from the words He speaks to the disciples in chapter 17. When Jesus heard the centurion declare his faith in Christ and in His power simply to *speak* healing into effect, rather than asking for an actual visit or a physical touch from Christ, Jesus "was amazed and said to those who followed him, 'Truly I tell you, in no one in Israel have I found such faith'" (8:10). What a blow to the disciples! A little later, after healing a father's epileptic son through an actual visit and a physical touch on the boy, Jesus rebukes the disciples again, but this time with a bit of advice: "For truly I tell you, if you have faith the size of a mustard seed, you will say to this mountain, 'Move from here to there,' and it will move; and nothing will be impossible for you" (17:20).

Jesus tries to make abundantly clear to His disciples in both instances that faith, by definition, must move us beyond what we can see and touch. A true mustard seed faith can, in fact, invoke God's grace and power simply through the spoken word. This faith applied to our dramatic gifts may renew our understanding of drama's symbolic power to minister and may help us relinquish our dependence on the spectacular to the wonderful mystery and irony of God's creative clarity through human artistic expression.

## Context (Questions for Reflection or Discussion):

*What are some ways in which our faith, like that of the disciples in Matt. 17, is lacking when we prepare a drama production? How was the centurion's faith in Matt. 8 different from that of the epileptic boy's father in chapter 17? Which kind of faith does Christ expect from us in the drama ministry at our church?*

## Suggestions for Prayer:

- A growing faith among our team members that is based on the "evidence of things not seen"
- A deeper trust in God in response to our obedience to Him
- A better understanding of symbolism in the theatre and how it speaks more powerfully than depiction

# . . . And Gestus for All

---
K
---

> "We must preach the Gospel in all that we do,
> and if we need to, use words."
> —Francis of Assisi

## Text:

"But be doers of the word, and not merely hearers who deceive themselves. For if any are hearers of the word and not doers, they are like those who look at themselves in a mirror; for they look at themselves and, on going away, immediately forget what they were like. But those who look into the perfect law, the law of liberty, and persevere, being not hearers who forget but doers who act—they will be blessed in their doing" (James 1:22-25).

## Subtext:

The actor was actually an administrator at a small Christian, liberal arts college in New England. But he had a love for drama and a gift for performing it. So, in costume and unrecognizable to students, he walked onto the platform one chapel morning and began an unforgettable, original, 20-minute monologue in the character of Judas. The portrayal was agonizing and complex, bringing to light the great human conflict and spiritual pain hidden away in the life of one of Jesus' most devout disciples.

At first, the motion was almost imperceptible—a slight wiping of the mouth. As the monologue continued, however, the gesture became more frequent and more intense until Judas was rubbing his lips after every sentence. Finally, the actor completed the picture for the audience by revealing in his lines how Judas's lips had not stopped burning since he had kissed Jesus in Gethsemane. The gesture had now evolved into more than mere physical action, taking on an entirely new, symbolic meaning. What a powerful image! What a compelling "gestus"!

A *gestus?* It's a term worth a closer look.

The plays and production styles of the remarkable 20th-century German playwright and director Bertolt Brecht have helped define much of the modern theatre as we know it today. He introduced groundbreaking concepts to the stage such as the intrusive narrator, epic theatre, and alienation (or *verfremdüngseffekt* in German, which is fun to say and sometimes impresses easily impressed friends at church gatherings). There is even an organization devoted solely to the work and philosophies of Brecht, known as the International Brecht Society.

Nevertheless, one of Brecht's methods of working with actors that is perhaps more useful for character development than some of his other practices is the notion of the *gestus*. The term is similar to our word *gesture* but is loaded with more meaning. In fact, in many ways, *gestus* contradicts the heavy, psychological acting

31

approach created by Stanislavsky in Russia. According to John Willett (translator for most of Brecht's theories), Brecht describes gestus as a combination of "gist and gesture; an attitude or a single aspect of an attitude, expressible in words and actions." In other words, a character may have a stance, a walk, a vocal inflection, a facial expression, or some other means of recognition that instantly defines for the audience the character's attitude or personality trait.

For instance, if a person were to quiver one side of his top lip and gyrate his thigh, we wouldn't need to hear the indelible words "thank you, thank you very much" to recognize Elvis. Other examples might include a wide receiver's signature touchdown victory dance, a mother's kneeling figure at her child's bedside, a single adult Sunday School teacher's distinctive laugh, the Scarecrow's flimsy carriage in *The Wizard of Oz*, Mister Rogers's pleasantly predictable shoe-sweater ritual, and Neil Armstrong's small step from the *Eagle*—all suggest varying types and degrees of the gestus in action.

Gestus, as we might see it onstage, can become a quick, powerful way to capture character and emotion economically within one definitive, symbolic silhouette, tableau, or movement. A lot may be communicated about a person's attitude or personality—through a chronic cough, a hunched posture, or a burning mouth. Simply coach actors at rehearsal to illustrate what their character wants, feels, or who the character is, and a repeatable gestus is bound to emerge along the way.

## Context (Questions for Reflection or Discussion):

*We hear these words too often: "If we talk the talk, we should walk the walk." But what does it really mean to walk the walk? What is the walk, exactly? How do our behaviors with each other at rehearsal or in the wings during a presentation define us in the eyes of our peers? in the eyes of those to whom we are ministering?*

Yet for all of its value as a character and storytelling device, does Brecht's gestus concept ever creep into our actual life offstage and affect our own spiritual growth? Sure it does. God's written Word tells us over and over again that we are known by our actions. "Even children make themselves known by their acts," says the proverb (Prov. 20:11). Known by our acts—hey, that's a gestus!

In fact, every Christian has a *spiritual* gestus or two—some distinct action or behavior that immediately identifies his or her unique personal relationship with Christ. Over a period of time, as this behavior repeats itself into a pattern, the cloud of witnesses that watch us naturally begin to make spiritual associations and assumptions about us, "for each tree is known by its own fruit" (Luke 6:44).

## Context (Questions for Reflection or Discussion):

*If others look to us as spiritual role models because of the drama ministry team, and if we acknowledge each other as partners in Christ, how can we know whether the gestus that others may identify with us offstage is a Christlike one?*

What is my spiritual gestus? That's a good question. Is it greeting and shaking hands with the elderly from pew to pew every Sunday morning before the service? Could it possibly be high-fiving and hugging the kids each summer in VBS?

Maybe it's a weekly card, phone call, or visit of encouragement to someone in the church family who is struggling with a personal loss.

How about our spiritual gestus within the fellowship of our own drama ministry team? Would it be an authentic word of caring spoken to our least favorite team member before each rehearsal? Is it an unfailing attentiveness to our director's artistic instruction and spiritual sensitivity? Perhaps we regularly offer a fresh cup of coffee and a helping hand to the overworked costume designers of our Christmas musical.

## Context (Questions for Reflection or Discussion):

*What can we do realistically to avoid making false assumptions and prejudgments about others based on their habitual behavior?*

Sometimes when a person is observing someone else we hear him or her reply in surprise, "My sister does that too!" or "That's a classic Bobby!" or "What a [fill in the person's name] thing to do!" So what kinds of actions do we want associated with us? What kinds of meaning do we want attached by others to *our* patterns of behavior? Is there a gestus you'd like to be known for or remembered by in your drama group? in your church? in your family? in your relationship with the Father? Gestus isn't about fooling other people. Brecht says that gestus is the recurrent, outward manifestation of an inward condition. What does our spiritual gestus say about our condition in Christ?

## Context (Questions for Reflection or Discussion):

*How can we better support each other in our drama ministry team using a gestus concept? What are some ways we can move beyond simply hearing and also become doers in our group? What in our relationship with God changes when we walk away from the mirror and "forget what we are like" (as the scripture text suggests)?*

## Suggestions for Prayer:
- That our actions and behaviors might more accurately reflect our own personal relationship with Christ
- Effective, life-changing ministry created through memorable characterizations and the use of gestus

# "All of You Wonderful People in the Dark"

---
P
---

"Every now and then, when you're onstage, you hear the best sound
a player can hear. It's a sound you can't get in movies or in television.
It is the sound of a wonderful, deep silence that means you've
hit them where they live."
—Shelley Winters

## Text:

"We declare to you what we have seen and heard so that you also may have fellowship with us; and truly our fellowship is with the Father and with his Son Jesus Christ" (1 John 1:3).

## Subtext:

Many of us know Patrick Stewart best as Captain Picard in *Star Trek: The Next Generation*. But not as many fans may recognize him as a highly trained Shakespearean actor who has spent years performing in the Royal Shakespeare Company at Stratford-upon-Avon. In 1997, while performing the role of Othello in Washington, D.C., Stewart spoke about the unique nature of theatre at a luncheon of the National Press Club.

In his speech, he suggested that the event of performance is a *contract* between the artists and the audience who have come together for two or more hours to share a common experience. According to Stewart, the promise of the actor is to take the audience on a journey—to show them "the human heart, in all its tenderness, its cruelty, its pain, its absurdity" and to promise them "the possibility of an experience that might stay with [them] for life." The audience's promise to the actors, he claims, is simpler: "Don't bore us, and we promise to put the next 2, 3, 4, 5, 6 hours of our precious time into your hands."

Most drama ministry teams experience a similar mutual expectation on both sides of the footlights. The congregation comes to the sanctuary or fellowship hall anticipating a drama ministry event that will be entertaining, compelling, and spiritually significant, with the promise of their undivided attention as a result. In return, the team promises to give them an experience that will find their audience afterward not the same one that sat down in the pews, but one that has been renewed and challenged in the Holy Spirit. The relationship, in a sense, is not simply a contract, but an unspoken covenant.

## Context (Questions for Reflection or Discussion):

*How do covenant and communion in Christ manifest themselves in our drama ministry at our church? List several tangible ways we can foster a deeper spirit of communion between our drama team and our church audience in performance.*

The shaping of this covenant relationship is an evanescent one. Every live moment in the theatre between the actor and the audience is fleeting and "in the now" and can never really be recovered afterward (which helps to explain why videotaped copies of past productions so poorly capture the live spirit of performances). The *communal* theatrical experience is one that cannot be duplicated—unlike film and television events—because the audience, the atmosphere, and the live actors' performances are all slightly different from night to night.

Stewart explains, too, that the theatrical experience is one that can never really be fully rehearsed, because the other vital half of that experience—namely, the audience—never shows up until the first performance. Consequently, every performance is a sort of gamble or *risk*. No one is really quite sure what will happen next. Like athletes in a cheering crowd, we thrive on theatre's spontaneity and the energy of the audience when they are there.

Although these descriptions of performance are true for theatre in general, perhaps they best describe what happens in Spirit-driven, life-changing drama ministry: there is a promise of *covenant*, an act of *communion*, a sense of *risk*. When these three qualities come together, they interact delicately and usually nourish the soul in a very personal, indescribable way. Used carelessly, however, they can carry with them a potential to produce unhealthy friction in worship or fellowship.

A contemporary retelling of the parable of the prodigal son, for example, may depict our modern prodigal abusing the financial and emotional support of his parents while away at college. He parties, he drinks, he buckles under sexual temptation. His sinful behavior may go undiluted onstage so that the powerful, redemptive grace of his parents' love upon his return is not minimized near the end of the story.

However, after the service, we may also discover that we have unintentionally offended some of the highly respected pillars among our laity. They are upset at the portrayal of a young man carousing with his dorm buddies. In fact, they may resent the mere suggestion of drugs and beer bottles (albeit props) in the sanctuary. They are incensed and take some of their righteous anger out on us.

Assuming our productions are prayerfully scripted and tastefully performed, how do we respond to our brothers and sisters in Christ? Have we, in fact, misread our target audience and perhaps inadvertently violated our covenant with them? How do we demonstrate a compassion for our church family without losing our passion for the incarnational ministry of the enacted Word?

## Context (Questions for Reflection or Discussion):

*What would be our response to a situation similar to the one described concerning the present-day prodigal son presentation? What are some examples of mistakes we have made in the past regarding content, approach, and sensitivity, and how have we learned and improved from those mistakes?*

All theatre organizations, regardless of mission or location, have a target audience in mind when they plan their productions. We must always keep ours in mind as well, with no apology. If we can challenge our audiences in provocative ways without offending them (or even pushing the boundaries, for that matter), we have achieved a higher level of artistic and ministerial finesse, and true communion can take place. But sometimes we confuse the cutting edge with the bleeding edge! Fellowship beyond the footlights cannot be nurtured unless the actor-audience contract remains unbroken. And because "truly our fellowship is with the Father and with his Son Jesus Christ," our covenant in performance takes on eternal significance! This covenant is not to be treated lightly.

On several wrenching occasions in Andrew Lloyd Webber's *Sunset Boulevard*, the faded silent film star Norma Desmond madly reminisces the glory days of her career as a movie star. Two of the most powerful instances of her delusional nostalgia show her remembering her fans of yesteryear and calling them by name—"all of you wonderful people in the dark"—as she squints past the lights and waves her hand across the auditorium. By doing so, she brings the actual theatre audience into the imaginary world of the play through a brilliant bit of theatrical convention. In essence, the included theatre audience has instantly become a character from Norma's past. It is chilling to be in the audience at that moment.

Although we don't normally seek that kind of effect in performance dramatically, our desire *should* be to include our audience in a similar way spiritually and relationally—a unique covenantal, communal fellowship in which God inspires and challenges all of us to be the growing, acting Body of Christ.

### Context (Questions for Reflection or Discussion):

*Who is our target audience exactly? What are they like? Which language and imagery speaks to them most effectively?*

### Suggestions for Prayer:

- For true communion to emerge among our drama ministry team, our church audience, our Father and Christ Jesus in every performance
- To recognize God's sovereign discernment in providing challenge and inspiration to our audience without offending them
- To know the collective needs of our church audience and to be Christlike in our sensitivity to those needs in performance

# I Second That Emotion

## K

"All emotions are pure which gather you and lift you up; that emotion is impure which seizes only *one* side of your being and so distorts you."
—Rainer Maria Rilke

**Text:**

"Rejoice with those who rejoice, weep with those who weep" (Rom. 12:15).

**Subtext:**

Ever glimpsed a forest just after an ice storm? The sight is stunning—a gorgeous, crystalline maze of branches and boughs glistening in the winter sun beneath a crisp veneer of ice; an infinite palace of glass reaffirming God's majesty and inimitable creativity.

Despite the unforgettable beauty of these frozen trees, many of them do not stand upright. Some of them bend over only slightly while others slump all the way to the ground. Why is it that some trees appear disfigured by the ice while others remain unaffected?

The stalwart victors are the trees who have already released most of their leaves. The sagging and collapsed trees, on the other hand, are those still clinging to their autumn costumes. When the storm hits and the ice accumulates, the trees with the most leaves ironically receive the greatest burden of ice, becoming deformed in the process. Sadly, these stubborn timbers have refused to let go of their otherwise-light loads under the weight of the storm.

Powerful negative emotions seem to affect us in much the same way. For actors and directors in rehearsal, the situation can become chronic and disruptive in at least three ways. The first is the actor (or director) who enters the rehearsal time with emotional baggage from the day at work or at home and can't seem to shake it off. Someone in this state of mind will remain preoccupied and self-conscious for the duration of rehearsal, making the group's time together somewhat counterproductive.

A second way that emotions can drag a team down takes the form of unresolved conflict within the group itself. Ironically, as the saying goes, "Without conflict there can be no drama." Whoever coined that insight, however, meant to describe conflict among the characters, not among the actors!

## Context (Questions for Reflection or Discussion):

*How does our director handle the feelings and emotions of preoccupied actors/tech members in rehearsal when those emotions seem to be counterproductive to our time together? How do those of us in the cast or technical crew respond in Christlike support to our director and to troubled actors/tech members during such times?*

Third, we consider Stanislavsky again, and his emotion memory recall approach to realistic acting. Using this approach, Stanislavsky asked that his actors emotionally relive a moment from their pasts that resembled a similar situation in the immediate life of the character they were playing. Unfortunately, after having used that method for years with his actors, he gradually came to discover how psychologically damaging this kind of intensely realistic scene work was for many of his actors. They were coming unglued, breakdown after breakdown.

Has our drama team ever attempted emotion memory recall to heighten the credibility in our actors' performances? Probably not. On the other hand, have we ever experienced the first two scenarios? Most likely. Our drama ministry team members may effortlessly handle their inward feelings and their emotions (the outward manifestations of those inward feelings) *most* of the time. But what happens to our group when the "masters of emotion" allow their emotions to master them?

Professional directors will not tolerate the first scenario for very long. Nor should we. But rather than scolding our brothers and sisters in the Body of Christ when they bring their baggage to rehearsal, we need instead to pay attention to their emotions without reading into them unduly. We need to be sensitive and to inquire, discreetly and privately, into the causes for their distracting behavior. If they seem to open up through the voluntary disclosure of their frustrations or struggles, either individually or in the embrace of the entire team's fellowship, it is time for sensitivity, compassion, and authentic prayer to take over rehearsal for a while.

True, we are giving up valuable rehearsal time, which is always at a premium in the midst of busy schedules. But what is *most* valuable, after all? Are we to forego the nurturing and nourishment of one another's spirit when the Holy Spirit elects to intervene? If we have faithfully allowed God to mold our goals according to His design, doesn't He promise to get us there in *His* time?

## Context (Questions for Reflection or Discussion):

*How do we balance a sensitivity to the needs represented within our group with the need to be productive in rehearsal? Is it up to us or to our director to draw the lines on how we use our rehearsal time? Why or why not?*

Resolving internal conflict within our team is even more difficult and time-consuming. Personality conflicts or careless horseplay can lead into some of the most dangerous tension. Jesus dealt with those very problems among His disciples all the time. He was constantly realigning their hearts. How can we learn to turn our emotions over to Him and to trust Him with them?

Although every circumstance is unique, proper, equitable communication is always the first step in working toward resolution. A healthy working relationship among team members means that we can *agree to disagree* without our emotions taking over. We must learn to channel our feelings in positive, constructive ways and to handle our emotions wisely.

Charlton Heston has been quoted as saying that the mind is more important than the body in the art of acting, for the mind controls everything else. Yet so many times it seems that our emotions control our minds. If that is true, then it becomes imperative that we allow our relationship with Christ to govern our emotions.

## Context (Questions for Reflection or Discussion):

*List some ways our team can negotiate rehearsal time and resolve conflicts more effectively in the short time we have together. How can we better implement the philosophy of agreeing to disagree in our regular encounters with one another? How does the Holy Spirit's active participation during rehearsal help us deal with our human emotions more responsibly?*

## Suggestions for Prayer:

- Maximum rehearsal time and space for the team and schedule availability of team members
- Patience, sensitivity, and discernment concerning the emotional needs of team members
- Those among our team who are emotionally, physically, and/or spiritually distraught

# Pardon Me, but Your Subtext Is Showing

## K

"Words don't have meaning. People do."
—Marshall McLuhan

**Text:**

"Pilate asked him, 'So you are a king?' Jesus answered, 'You say that I am a king. For this I was born, and for this I came into the world, to testify to the truth. Everyone who belongs to the truth listens to my voice.' Pilate asked him, 'What is truth?'" (John 18:37-38).

**Subtext:**

Most of us probably know what the crew of the *Titanic* did not. That, as with most icebergs, the portion of ice they could see above the water was deceptively small in comparison to the hulking mass of ice suspended in the dark beneath the ocean's surface. Lee Strasberg, the infamous 20th-century director and acting teacher, was known to have likened all human interaction to such an iceberg. Like icebergs, each of us has a very small portion of ourselves visible above the surface of our public self—perhaps roughly only 10 to 15 percent. The other 85 to 90 percent of ourselves lies lurking beneath the surface.

The part above the water he described as our text, while the larger mass beneath he referred to as subtext. And it is surprising how often subtext finds its way into our ordinary interactions with others every day. When we reprimand or reward our pets, for instance, they are more likely to understand our communication through the inflections in our voices than through the actual words we say. We could angrily yell "Good dog!" or "Good kitty!" at our furry companions, and the words wouldn't mean a thing as they proceed to cower anyway. Ironically, E-mail has done the opposite in human quarters! We most often receive a hastily written text with very little understanding of the tone or inflection that might normally accompany that speaker's voice. Enter confusion! Paralanguage (or the lack thereof) can be a most disturbing, yet necessary phenomenon in human communication.

Likewise, realistic drama depends specifically on subtext for success. Nearly every script written in the last 150 years contains dialogue that is considered by teacher Francis Hodge to be a mere facade. The real meaning behind what is being said is tucked away underneath the dialogue. The actor's and director's jobs, of course, are to dig out clues in the dialogue that reveal the exact subtext beneath the facade of the text so that both may be carefully enacted onstage in the storytelling process.

## Context (Questions for Reflection or Discussion):

*How does one go about finding the subtext in a script? How much weight should we give stage directions as clues to subtext?*

In this sense, drama makes a valiant effort at imitating life. We use text and subtext all the time. In fact, we find ourselves in trouble most of the time when we do not say exactly what we mean. (Can we ever?) On other occasions, we might tell a friend how nice her new dress or jacket looks when, in fact, we are only being kind. The incongruities of text and subtext are frequently the substance of great comedy as well. The distinguished communication theorist Marshall McLuhan perhaps summarized subtext best when he claimed that "words don't have meaning; people do." The external signs and symbols we call language are only crude representations of our internal meanings.

## Context (Questions for Reflection or Discussion):

*How is it possible that words don't really have meaning? Try to recall some instances from our own experiences, either in rehearsal or out, in which some significant misunderstanding took place between ourselves and someone else simply due to confusion between text (what was said) and subtext (what was meant). What guidance does Scripture offer in the way of avoiding such confusion in the future?*

Therefore, as disciples of Christ (and especially as practitioners of theatre) we are responsible for learning how to read carefully between the lines, onstage and off, without being presumptuous or intrusive. The practice of reading subtext in scripts, in Scripture, and in our personal conversations with other people is basic to our understanding of human interaction and of God's active participation in our lives. We look for subtextual clues when we analyze a play script. We unpack scriptural texts to see what has been tucked away for us within the Word of God. We search people's faces and read their subtlest expressions to increase our sensitivity and Christlike responsiveness to their hidden hurts and unspoken needs. Jesus' words throughout the Gospels reveal His own preference for the subtextual: questions, parables, and warnings. ("The reason I speak to them in parables is that 'seeing they do not perceive, and hearing they do not listen, nor do they understand'" [Matt. 13:13]. Read *all* of chapter 13 for a thorough review of the eternal significance of subtext in Jesus' ministry!)

Does *our* drama ministry team make a habit of carefully reading subtext? How do we do it or become better at it? Why is it so important to our spiritual health that we be able to discern the subtext of our life stories? May God empower us with the capacity to read not only *between* the lines of script, scripture, and daily conversation but also *beyond* those lines so that we might perceive and listen more clearly as God reveals His mystery and majesty to us in His time.

## Context (Questions for Reflection or Discussion):

*We know the text of our lives very well. What is God's subtext for our lives? What can we see He is really doing in us if we read our lives between and beyond the lines?*

## Suggestions for Prayer:

- A carefully developed skill for detecting subtext in scripts in order to enrich our interpretations of characters and stories onstage
- The ability to discern subtext more clearly in our interactions with others in our church and team
- A better vision of God's subtext for our own lives and ways we can become more effective "readers" of our own subtext

# Send in the . . . Clones?

K

> "Though all men be made of one metal,
> yet they be not cast all in one mold."
> —John Lyly, Elizabethan playwright

## Text:

"But as it is, God arranged the members in the body, each one of them, as he chose. If all were a single member, where would the body be? As it is, there are many members, yet one body" (1 Cor. 12:18-20).

## Subtext:

As the story goes, the celebrated painter Michelangelo was once approached by a fascinated onlooker who was clearly in awe of his most recent masterpiece—the statue of *David*. The observer asked Michelangelo how he was able to carve such a magnificent figure that had all the detail of humanity, yet projected a marvelous three-dimensional image that was larger than life. In response, Michelangelo explained that he had examined the giant block of uncut marble for a long time until he clearly saw David inside the rock. When he was through looking, he simply chiseled away everything in the uncut stone that was not David, and by the time he was done, the statue was left standing by itself, finally freed from captivity.

Many of the best acting coaches and teachers will take time to show young performers how to develop a character and its portrayal onstage beyond the mere two-dimensional caricature so common among beginning actors. They will frequently use the helpful metaphor of the onion to illustrate how a character, like every real individual, has many layers of experience, personality, and meaning; every character is multilayered or multidimensional.

While this is true and serves as an important approach to character study, it is also true that characters are not created in a vacuum. Every actor makes a significant contribution to the life of the character portrayed from his or her own personal layers of experience, personality, and meaning. Every actor has his or her own private audiences and public self, both of which figure prominently into the end product of characterization in performance. Whereas the first approach to character development is additive in that the actor adds layers and nuances on top of a character (based on clues from the script), this second way of looking at character may be termed *subtractive acting*, or *personalization*, because it urges actors to find personal connections between their own experiences and personalities and those of their characters.

## Context (Questions for Reflection or Discussion):

*What are some roles we have played in which we discovered several personal connections with the character? How were those connections expressed to the audience during the performance of these characters?*

Actors might be viewed, then, as large blocks of uncut stone containing a wealth of individual human experiences, memories, feelings, and ideas. Like Michelangelo chiseling away at *David,* actors may create very detailed, very credible characters that are still larger than life by sculpting their inner selves and carving away anything they do not personally have in common with their characters. What is left is a unique combination of the character and the actor—an amalgam that no other actor will ever be able to duplicate precisely. For all of Hamlet's notoriety, every portrayal of Hamlet must, in fact, be unique by default: the Olivier Hamlet, the Welles Hamlet, the Gibson Hamlet, the Brannagh Hamlet. How intriguing! No portrayal is ever the same!

This diversity in the development of character is cause for celebration! Not only does it hold the promise of original and provocative performances of plays we have already seen time and time again, but it also reaffirms our Father's abundant creativity and generosity in His distribution of expressive gifts among His children.

We represent an infinite menagerie of artistic strengths and weaknesses. Let us celebrate our God-given strengths, using them to glorify the Giver, and champion the unique contributions each actor, director, or designer has to bring to the table in rehearsal and in performance. Ironically, if we applaud and uphold our drama ministry team members in this way, we seldom find ourselves wishing we could do what everyone else seems to do so well. Insecurities and self-serving envy melt away, and a jubilee of Christlike esteem and mutual admiration ignites.

## Context (Questions for Reflection or Discussion):

*How frequently do we compare our roles and/or performances with those of other actors? What are some meaningful ways we can acknowledge the merits of one another's unique abilities without being self-indulgent?*

Even as we honor one another's special abilities and unique interpretive strengths, however, we are called to keep our vision in perspective. Imagine what would happen if we were to keep our eyes focused on another member of our drama ministry team as the sole or primary object of our admiration. If they were to go off the tracks for any reason, we would be pulled off in that direction right along with them. Ultimately, we are called to fix our eyes on Christ, the author and perfecter of our faith.

Subtractive acting contains a fundamental spiritual premise. As we strive to become more and more like Christ every day, we must let God chip away at every chunk and sliver of sin that is not a part of the Christlike individual He has originally intended for us to be. And we must, with faith and obedience, learn to be willing to accept the role He has given us to perform within the larger Body of Christ. Let us give credit to whom credit is due and thank God for wonderfully, mysteriously fashioning us after His own image!

## Context (Questions for Reflection or Discussion):

*What do we perceive as our individual roles within our drama ministry team, both artistically and personally? Are we willing to allow God to place us in another role or position of responsibility should He so desire? Looking back, in what ways has He already sculpted us in preparation for the ministerial and artistic roles we are in right now?*

## Suggestions for Prayer:

- Genuine respect for one another's God-ordained gifts and talents
- A willingness to be shaped into the Christlike, yet unique individuals God has intended us to be from the outset

# The Grand Illusion

---
P
---

"I read in a periodical the other day that the fundamental thing is how we
think of God. By God Himself, it is not! How God thinks of us is not only
more important, but infinitely more important. Indeed, how we think of Him
is of no importance except in so far as it is related to how He thinks of us."
—C. S. Lewis, *The Weight of Glory*

## Text:

"Anyone who claims to know something does not yet have the necessary
knowledge; but anyone who loves God is known by him" (1 Cor. 8:2-3).

## Subtext:

When Konstantin Stanislavsky proclaimed that "great art is art concealed," he
was not referring to stolen paintings. What he did mean by that remark is that the
best craftsmanship (acting, directing, design, etc.) in theatre should be so convinc-
ing that we as audience members lose ourselves in it completely. We temporarily
forget that what we are watching is, in fact, only a play.

If the actors are well-trained and their characters jump out at us, what we ob-
serve appears to be real. In other words, the actors are *so* credible when they cry,
argue, or bubble with laughter that we forget they are indeed acting.

Likewise, if a designer has done his or her job par excellence with scenery or
costumes, then the skill or artistry should never bring undue attention to itself.
We should not actually see the wires or the genie lift in the ascension scene. We
should not actually see the fog machine at the mouth of the empty tomb. We
should not actually see the safety pins and spirit gum holding the actors, sometimes quite delicately, together.

If we are truly artful, and if our congregation is familiar with drama as an art
and as a ministry, there will be a sense among artist and audience alike that we
are all experiencing something authentic and compelling for a brief moment in
time. Poet/playwright Samuel Taylor Coleridge refers to this activity as the "willing
suspension of disbelief." We come together, and for 15 or 30 or 90 minutes we voluntarily accept the grand illusion of the theatre for something that is real and very
personal to us.

## Context (Questions for Reflection or Discussion):

*How can our drama ministry team do a better job of "concealing" our art? How
can we shift attention away from the obvious residues of acting, directing, and
design in performance so that audiences will forget the art but remember the
stories, characters, and themes themselves?*

This illusion, and its symbolism, is part of what makes the event of theatre so exhilarating and so powerful as a communicator of ideas. Theatre allows us to see parts of the world through the eyes of others without having to be in their shoes.

Yet, it is also this illusion that has for years caused many conservative Christians some concern. Should we be pretending to be someone else? Are Christians supposed to be "playacting"? After all, the Greek word *hypokrites* literally means "actor." Aren't we actually hypocrites with the repertoire of masks and disguises we haul around in our trunk? According to Stanislavsky, the more people we fool, the better actors we are. Is he right? And if so, is this how we wish others to think of us in drama ministry?

## Context (Questions for Reflection or Discussion):

*How do members of our church perceive theatre? In what ways is our church progressive, conservative, or both?*

Any analogy can be extended too far, obviously (and this one has been *often*). Fortunately, however, we know that ministry through drama is not about fooling people at all, but about honoring God's voice and creativity in the stories He's given us to share from other people's lives. Even so, there seems to linger at times a common misconception that this double life actors appear to lead (even those who are Christians) cannot be a healthy one. In many minds, imagination and simulation onstage are still confused with masquerade and pretense.

How then do we respond to this illusive paradox? First of all, as imitators of Christ, one of our most important responsibilities will always be *transparency*. When we are truly transparent Christians, we have allowed God to clean out our darkest personal closets and to open the blinds and shutters of our insecurities to the radiance of His redemptive grace. We have surrendered everything—our finances, our relationships, our failures, our aspirations, our pride—at the foot of the Cross and live a life fearlessly exposed to His love and unmasked before others.

Second, as creators of theatrical illusion, we specialize in distinguishing the real from the artificial. Although transparency in our daily witness is the natural product of a Spirit-filled life, it should also be an integral part of ministry in the performing arts. The stigma of pretense that is sometimes unfairly attached to those who perform in ministry is rapidly dispelled when we reveal ourselves genuinely broken and transparent in Christ. Are we able to remove our various disguises—macho man, career woman, perfect student, supermom, supreme tither, and so forth—as easily as we wear them in the first place?

C. S. Lewis points out (in what is arguably his most important writing, *The Weight of Glory*) that we usually fail to become transparent when we go "dressing up as Christ." We don the outward costume of Christlikeness instead of letting Christ honestly "turn [us] into the same kind of thing as Himself." In most cases, we spend so much time trying to know God that we fail to allow *ourselves to be known to Him.*

## Context (Questions for Reflection or Discussion):

*What does it mean to be transparent? What are some examples of spiritual transparency from our own experiences or from those of our families and friends? How does God reveal in Scripture some ways to let ourselves be known to Him?*

"Does not God know all things at all times?" teases Lewis. To be known by God means to be recognized by our inward attitudes and outward behavior as a servant of Christ, a child of the Father. It means to be laid out, broken, vulnerable, exposed nakedly to His awesome grace and redemptive love. It means, as Lewis suggests, to be *famous*—not in the eyes of men, but in God's eyes! It means relying upon that grace and love to live a life transparent before Him, that we might one day hear the words we long for: "Well done, thou good and faithful servant."

To be known by God, rather than to know God; to be welcomed, rather than refused in eternal horror by the words, "I never knew you. Depart from me"; to be embraced, rather than to be unspeakably ignored, Lewis says, is our perfect re-union with God, the restoration of creature to Creator—not merely an end to rationalize the means, but a fulfillment of our becoming Christlike.

Stanislavsky's words were profoundly correct when he warned us to avoid letting our art become transparent. Concealment must accompany the grand illusion of theatre in order for drama to do its job and to be "great" drama. Yet the greater, spiritual illusion we face every day may be our mistaken belief that knowing God is more important than letting ourselves be known by Him. Transparency, rather than concealment, must be one of the fruits of our personal relationship with Christ. And for the drama ministry team in particular, transparency in Christ should be a trademark.

## Context (Questions for Reflection or Discussion):

*What are we sacrificing when we choose to be transparent to God and to others around us? If transparency means discomfort and vulnerability for us, how do we overcome those feelings? Do we love Him enough to be known by Him intimately?*

## Suggestions for Prayer:

- Empowerment from God the Creator for excellence in dramatic art
- A genuine transparency in our team at all times, individually and collectively, that allows others to see Christ in us
- To be known and fully disclosed to God

# Go Ahead, Make My Deus Ex Machina

## K

"Without the assistance of that Divine Being, I cannot succeed.
With that assistance, I cannot fail."
—Abe Lincoln

**Text:**

"See, I am coming soon; my reward is with me, to repay according to everyone's work. I am the Alpha and the Omega, the first and the last, the beginning and the end" (Rev. 22:12-13).

**Subtext:**

Remember when we first heard Dorothy speak the magical words, "There's no place like home, there's no place like home"? It was as simple as that. With those comforting words and a few clicks of her ruby heels, Dorothy was suddenly able to leave behind nearly all of it: Munchkinland, the Wicked Witch's disturbing air-born primates, and even "the man behind the curtain." Almost two hours of adventure after adventure instantly dismissed into a delirious dream by an absurdly simple ritual. After all, *could* it have been anything else but a dream?

And who was responsible for letting Dorothy in on this convenient secret? Why none other than Glenda the Good Witch who drives a sporty, little bubble to get around. Good thing she didn't drop any clues to Dorothy way back at the beginning of the yellow brick road where the Lollipop Guild resides. The movie would have lasted only 20 minutes!

Fortunately, L. Frank Baum's story of *The Wizard of* Oz is so carefully constructed, so beautifully realized on camera, and so enchanting overall that we (particularly as children) readily accept the brilliant solution to bring Dorothy home on a little bit of magic and a lot of Auntie Em's smelling salts. However, we can probably think of several *poorly* written stories for film or for stage whose increasing plot twists and complications were suddenly, amazingly solved at the end of the story through the powerful, often miraculous intervention of a surprise visitor with some sort of special power or authority.

This phenomenon of bringing in a superhero character to save the day at the end of an otherwise hopelessly messy plot situation is known as *deus ex machina,* or literally "god out of machine." The term originated in the theatre of ancient Greece when Apollo, Athena, Zeus, or some other mostly benevolent Olympian god would literally descend from the heavens onstage to set all things right and return order to the land at the end of a play. The technique of lowering gods or other supernatural creatures from the heavens continued well into Shakespeare's time and eventually translated into the use of flying systems on larger proscenium stages in the centuries to follow.

Dramatically, deus ex machina has become a point of credibility in story-telling and scriptwriting. The famous comic French playwright Molière delighted in playfully including an emissary from King Louis XIV to save the day rather abruptly at the ends of some of his plays. Gilbert and Sullivan even poked fun at the silliness and unlikeliness of deus ex machina at the end of *The Pirates of Penzance* when Queen Victoria's appearance at the end of the operetta unexpectedly turns the tide of events in the plot. Film is even more susceptible than theatre. A classic example occurs in the science fiction movie *Star Wars* when, as Luke Skywalker prepares to deliver the final blow to Darth Vader's Death Star but is hopelessly surrounded by the enemy in space battle, his (almost forgotten) friend Han Solo suddenly appears out of nowhere from darkness and clears a path to victory! Use the force, Luke!

## Context (Questions for Reflection or Discussion):

*Name a few plays or movies that have abused the device of deus ex machina. What exactly contributes to the underlying success or failure of this particular device in a story? What are the inevitable implications for us in our own story-telling onstage based on these contributions?*

Naturally, there is a valuable playwriting lesson to be gleaned from all of this. As our drama ministry team works on creating new ideas and scripts for worship sketches, youth services, all-church dinners, and so on, we should be sensible about keeping plot developments, character relationships, and dialogue believable. We should avoid teasing credibility, or we may severely tax our audience's willingness to subscribe to the dramatic conflict and its resolution.

Ironically and thankfully, on a deeply personal and spiritual level, God has promised us that He will do every day precisely what the deus ex machina syndrome tells us stageworthy scripts should *not* do. His word in Scripture reveals His faithfulness to rescue us from ourselves at all times, if we are only willing to let Him. Our Father has historically proven himself to be especially active in the eleventh hour. Israel's passage through the Red Sea, Lazarus's resurrection, Jesus' calming of the storm before the frightened disciples—all seem to be relatively narrow escapes that, by human standards, were late in coming.

## Context (Questions for Reflection or Discussion):

*How do we respond to God's timing? Are we impatient? Do we get angry at God when He is quiet? Do we worry too much about God's control of our drama ministry, rather than trusting Him to pull us through as we faithfully focus on Him at the finish line?*

It is reassuring also to know that God's intervention in the fabric of our lives is no happy accident. Scripture illustrates for us how God's design is not mere whimsy, but a delicate plan with His creation's best interests in mind, despite the "groaning in labor pains" Paul so accurately attributes to our present condition.

So why do we still panic when a cast member quits the play two-thirds of the way into rehearsals or the set and costumes aren't quite finished before our final dress rehearsal? Why do we continue to throw our arms up in frustration when our pastoral staff or worship committees won't openly consider more creative approaches to worship on Sundays? Cannot God, without warning, do more than we had ever hoped or possibly imagined?

Although our cries for help to God are not meant to be manipulative, we sometimes fall into the trap of praying to Him only when we are in most need of assistance. What He asks of us is *our* faithfulness as well—our complete and utter dependence upon Him at *all* times throughout the remainder of our lives, not only during the desperate final moments of our most urgent dilemmas.

In the last act of humanity, God has promised the glorious, awesome, eternal deus ex machina for all of time! What a homecoming! Hallelujah! As we look forward to this future glory, Paul writes, we "groan inwardly while we wait for adoption, the redemption of our bodies" (Rom. 8:23). How then do we respond on a daily basis? Let us start by examining ourselves and our relationships with God, recognizing how He faithfully continues to intervene in our lives, even during our darkest hours.

## Context (Questions for Reflection or Discussion):

*What does Paul mean exactly when he writes to the Romans that we "groan inwardly while we wait"? In what ways can we more visibly demonstrate to God our complete dependence upon Him and our utter trust of His timing during our rehearsals and production work?*

## Suggestions for Prayer:

- The ability to identify and to avoid abuses of the deus ex machina device in scripts we encounter
- An ability to discern and to write our own scripts that contain solid dramatic writing and credible characters
- Appreciation for God's irony, sense of humor, flawless design, and simultaneous ability to comfort us in the loneliest times of our lives

# "What's Past Is Prologue"

## P

"Now this is not the end. It is not even the beginning of the end.
But it is, perhaps, the end of the beginning."
—Winston Churchill

### Text:

"Be on your guard, so that you do not lose what we have worked for, but may receive a full reward" (2 John 8).

### Subtext:

*The Tempest* is considered by many readers and critics to be one of William Shakespeare's finest plays as well as his swan song and farewell to a prolific career in playwriting. In the play, Prospero (often compared to the bard himself) rules the island and its grab bag of inhabitants with his powerful magic. At the play's end, however, he forgives his enemies, relinquishes his power, and retires from his world of lonely fatherhood and revenge to return to the natural world of the mainland. Antonio's words in Act 2 then are fitting for Prospero, Ariel, Miranda, and the others: "what's past is prologue." What has come before is only the beginning of the wonderful future that lies ahead.

Perseverance and continuity are two of the most important traits of an effective drama ministry team. What the team has already experienced together, learned in the way of dramatic ability and theatre prowess, and presented to audiences must be recycled into the future work and energy of the group. What our team has gained in taking time to share together, to grow closer relationally, and to commune with God devotionally during or outside of rehearsals must be nurtured and nourished on a consistent basis.

### Context (Questions for Reflection or Discussion):

*How might we successfully perpetuate the work that has begun in drama ministry team, both artistically and spiritually? How can we effectively divide our rehearsal time in such a way that we nourish our spirits as well as prepare ourselves theatrically?*

Effective actors innovatively explore their roles all through the rehearsal process, gradually setting in stone the interpretive choices that seem to work best over a period of time. By the time they reach dress rehearsals and performances, their goal is usually no longer exploration, but rather *consistency*. They want to preserve what is working well in their performance, eliminate distractions that will cause them to lose focus, and thoroughly satisfy the role that has been bestowed upon them by their director.

Effective drama ministry teams can and should operate in similar fashion:

preserving strengths, curing weaknesses, eliminating distractions, and fulfilling our responsibilities to our church and community. Perhaps the greatest threat to most drama ministry teams is individual (and collective) burnout or lack of longevity. As a group works together over a period of many weeks, months, even years, several things begin to happen. The mission statement of the team may be lost to other projects and requests coming in from all sides. Group relationships may be strained, violated, or simply deteriorated with the prolonged familiarity and exposure to one another required by such an intensive ministry. Rehearsal time often becomes an even rarer commodity.

## Context (Questions for Reflection or Discussion):

*Are there any relationships in our team that are in need of healing right now? Can we confess our differences openly and share in the reconciliation Christ has made available to us through His own sacrifice? Are we still on track with our original mission as a drama ministry team?*

In order for us to endure as artistic, intelligent, and spiritually attuned communicators of God's unfailing love and purposeful interaction in the lives of His people, we ought to pray for strength and wisdom, both to grow in our relationships with God and with one another *and* to remain steadfast in our ministerial worth. Let us persevere, and keep on keeping on! Let us become lifelong learners—not only students of life but students of drama, discovering and mastering as much as we can about the art of theatre and how God might use that knowledge and those skills to win another soul to Christ. Let us glorify God in our stability, in our determination, and in our unwavering sensitivity toward one another in the process of serving our Lord Christ Jesus wherever has planted us.

## Context (Questions for Reflection or Discussion):

*How can we remain students of life and students of drama? In what ways can we further qualify ourselves to be called directors, designers, theatre technicians, and actors? Are there any additional ways we can revitalize our artistic and spiritual energies individually and as a group?*

## Suggestions for Prayer:
- The healing of damaged or strained relationships within our own drama ministry team
- Renewed focus on the original mission God set before us as a team
- Desire to learn more about drama and its potential for use as a ministry to meet the needs of others and to share the gospel with them

# Suggested Further Scripture Reading by Devotional

Below are some additional passages of Scripture that may prove particularly meaningful should you decide to spend some additional time with one or more of the devotionals in the book. These verses have been prayerfully selected to supplement the material in each of the devotionals to which they have been assigned. I pray that the Lord will use each of them to bless and to nourish you and the work of your team.

### Devotional: "What's My Motivation?"

Additional Scripture: Pss. 32:8; 119:105; Prov. 3:5-6; Isa. 30:20-21; John 16:13; Acts 5:38-39; James 1:5-8

### Devotional: Fast-Food Drama Ministry

Additional Scripture: Prov. 2:4-7; Isa. 42:16; John 15:2, 5; Phil. 1:6; Heb. 6:11-12; 10:35-36; 2 Pet. 1:9-10

### Devotional: Prima Donna 101

Additional Scripture: Mic. 6:6-8; Matt. 20:25-28; Luke 18:9-14; 2 Cor. 12:9-10; Gal. 6:3; Phil. 2:1-11

### Devotional: You Don't Bring Me Backdrops Anymore

Additional Scripture: Matt. 6:25-33; Mark 9:23-24; Rom. 8:28; 2 Cor. 4:18; Heb. 11:1-3

### Devotional: . . . And Gestus for All

Additional Scripture: Prov. 20:11; Matt. 7:20; Luke 6:46; John 3:21; Col. 3:17; Titus 1:16; 1 John 3:18

### Devotional: "All of You Wonderful People in the Dark"

Additional Scripture: Ps. 133:1; Matt. 18:20; Mark 9:50; Rom. 12:4-5; 1 Cor. 10:17; Eph. 4:25; 1 John 1:6-7

### Devotional: I Second That Emotion

Additional Scripture: Ps. 97:11; Prov. 15:13; 25:28; Eccles. 7:3; John 16:20; James 3:1-12

### Devotional: Pardon Me, but Your Subtext Is Showing

Additional Scripture: Matt. 13; John 3:1-12; 8:21-30

### Devotional: Send in the . . . Clones?

Additional Scripture: Ps. 139; 1 Cor. 12; 15:10

### Devotional: The Grand Illusion

Additional Scripture: Jer. 23:23-28; Prov. 20:11; Matt. 6:5-6; John 3:21; 4:24; 1 Cor. 3:18-20; Titus 1:16; 1 John 2:4-6

## Devotional: Go Ahead, Make My Deus Ex Machina

Additional Scripture: 2 Kings 17:39; Pss. 23; 46:1; Isa. 40:29-31; Matt. 18:20; Rom. 8:31

## Devotional: "What's Past Is Prologue"

Additional Scripture: Mark 2:21-22; 2 Cor. 5:17; Eph. 4:17-23; Col. 1:17; Heb. 3:4

# Related Drama Resources by Devotional

Here are some (primarily) drama resources related to each of the devotional discussions in this book. You may find some of these suggestions helpful for continuing your study of the devotional topics beyond your rehearsal times together. Also, I have listed extra resources at the end that are designed to unify your group (adults, teens, or children) through the tools of improvisation and imagination.

## Devotional: "What's My Motivation?"

Some related drama resources:

*Producing and Directing Drama for the Church,* by Robert Rucker (Lillenas)
*Developing the Church Drama Ministry,* by Paul Miller (Lillenas)
*An Actor Prepares, Building a Character,* and *Creating a Role* (The A-B-C Series), by Konstantin Stanislavsky
*Acting Power,* by Robert Cohen

## Devotional: Fast-Food Drama Ministry

Some related drama resources:

*Incorporating Drama in Worship,* by Mike Gray (LILLENAS)
*Addicted to Mediocrity: Twentieth-Century Christians and the Arts,* by Franky Schaeffer
*The Liberated Imagination,* by Leland Ryken

## Devotional: Prima Donna 101

Some related drama resources:

*Body Language,* by Joe Lovitt (Lillenas)
*Under the Circumstances,* by Torry Martin (Lillenas)
*Respect for Acting,* by Uta Hagen

## Devotional: You Don't Bring Me Backdrops Anymore

Some related drama resources:

*Worshiping Through Drama,* by David H. Kehret (Lillenas)
Any of the Lillenas readers theatre scripts by Stoltz, Moore, Lewis, and Robey
*The Empty Space,* by Peter Brook

## Devotional: . . . And Gestus for All

Some related drama resources:

*These Truths Were Made for Walking,* by Martha Bolton (Lillenas)
*Walk a Mile in His Truths,* by Martha Bolton (Lillenas)
*The Cambridge Companion to Brecht,* by Peter Thomson and Glendyr Sacks (eds.)
*Brecht on Theatre,* by Bertolt Brecht (John Willett, trans. and ed.)

## Devotional: "All of You Wonderful People in the Dark"

Some related drama resources:

*I Am the Vine,* by James Bradford (Lillenas)
*The Word in Worship,* by Paul Miller and Jeff Wyatt (Lillenas)
Speech by Patrick Stewart (December 4, 1997), *National Press Club* (Distributed by Media Pulse [1-800-742-1983])
*Theatre Audiences,* by Susan Bennett

## Devotional: I Second That Emotion

Some related drama resources:

> *People like Us,* by Patricia Souder and Jana Carman (Lillenas)
> *Psychotherapy to Go,* by Steve Trott (Lillenas)
> *Acting for Real: Drama Therapy—Process, Technique, and Performance,*
>     by Renée Emunah
> *Acting Through Exercises,* by John Gronbeck-Tedesco

## Devotional: Pardon Me, but Your Subtext Is Showing

Some related drama resources:

> *Playwriting: A Study in Choices and Challenges,* by Paul McCusker (Lillenas)
> *Welcome to the Mustard Seed Café,* by Dean A. Kephart (Lillenas)
> *Parables Onstage,* by Jeannette Clift George (Lillenas)
> *Playwriting: From Formula to Form,* by Wm. M. Downs and Lou Anne Wright

## Devotional: Send in the . . . Clones?

Some related drama resources:

> *Making a Name for Myself,* by Jill Richardson (Lillenas)
> *The WWJD Playbook,* by Chuck Neighbors (Lillenas)
> *Setting the Actor Free,* by Ann Brebner

## Devotional: The Grand Illusion

Some related drama resources:

> *Reality Check,* by Martha Bolton (Lillenas)
> *This Is Your Life,* by Jan Peterson Ewen (Lillenas)
> *He's Got My Number,* by Hicks and Cohagan (Lillenas)
> *The Weight of Glory,* by C. S. Lewis

## Devotional: Go Ahead, Make My Deus Ex Machina

Some related drama resources:

> *Body, Mind, and Spirit,* by Jeff Smith (Lillenas)
> *Act and React,* by Kevin Stone (Lillenas)
> *History of the Theatre,* by Oscar G. Brockett

## Devotional: "What's Past Is Prologue"

Some related drama resources:

> *Acts of Worship,* by Jeff Wyatt with Paul M. Miller (Lillenas)
> Any of the volumes in the Lillenas Worship Drama Library
> *The Tempest,* by William Shakespeare

## Extra Resources for Group Work Through Improvisation and Imagination:

> *Just for the Play of It,* by Debbie Salter Goodwin (Lillenas)
> *The Little Book of Theatre Games,* by Jim Custer, Bob Hoose, and Gary Reed (Lillenas)
> *Improvisation for the Theatre,* by Viola Spolin
> *Interactive Acting,* by Jeff Wirth
> *Truth in Comedy,* by Charna Halpern, Del Close, and Kim "Howard" Johnson

# Glossary of Terms and People

**Brecht, Bertolt**

Twentieth-century German playwright and the major conceptual force of the epic theatre movement, which mixed narrative and dramatic techniques into new art forms. Brecht's uses of *gestus* and *verfremdüngseffekt* emphasized theatricality to keep audiences in the world of the theatre event, to educate them rather than entertain them, and to bring about social change.

**deus ex machina**

Literally, "god from [or 'out of'] machine," as when the actors playing Olympian gods in ancient Greek theatre would be lowered from the "heavens" in the *skene*, or "stage house." Because Euripides often made use of this device to resolve his plots quickly, the term has come to represent any contrived ending onstage or in film.

**emotion memory recall**

An approach to realistic acting begun by Konstantin Stanislavsky at the Moscow Art Theatre in the late 19th century and intensified by Lee Strasberg in the United States throughout the 20th century. The approach encourages actors psychologically to relive emotions from past experiences in order to replicate them for similar dramatic situations onstage.

**gestus**

A technique used by Bertolt Brecht to help actors create more clearly defined and highly stylized characters. Repeatable gestures are used as tools of quick character recognition and interpretation.

**heteroglossia**

Multiple, conflicting, or divergent voices, often speaking simultaneously.

**minimalism**

A style of theatre production that imaginatively suggests, rather than depicts, the world of the play by using only the least number of carefully selected props, set pieces, and/or costume accessories needed to tell the story onstage.

**motivation**

In realistic forms of acting, what an actor determines to be the primary cause(s) for his or her character's action in a play. Motivation often deals with past experiences in a character's life as driving forces of behavior. Motivation is similar to, but not the same as, "intention," which implies a goal or desire for something in the future, rather than a driving force from the past.

**prima donna**

Literally, "first lady"; anyone wishing to be the center of attention onstage and off.

### Stanislavsky, Konstanin

Cofounder of the famous Moscow Art Theatre and world-famous director/acting teacher. He is most remembered for his renowned Method acting approach and his many attempts to perfect a technique or specific skill training for acting.

### Strasberg, Lee

Student of Stanislavsky and cofounder of the Group Theatre in the 1930s. He became a commanding force at the Actors Studio upon his arrival in the late 1940s, focusing more intensely on emotion memory recall and probing actors' inner thoughts/feelings as ways of revealing truth in performance.

### subtext

Hidden meaning or paralanguage that lies beneath the lines of a dialogue and that frequently contradicts the text of the dialogue itself; what we *really* mean when we say something.

### subtractive acting

Similar to personalization, this approach to preparing a role involves the actor finding as many personal connections as possible with his or her character's own life and building on those connections while, at the same time, stripping away other actor traits and idiosyncrasies that the actor does not share in common with the character.

### upstaging

The process of one actor stealing an audience's visual focus away from other actors onstage simply by positioning himself or herself farther upstage than the others, thereby forcing them to address that actor by turning away from the audience.

### willing suspension of disbelief

A phrase (usually attributed to poet and critic Samuel Taylor Coleridge) that describes an audience's decision to accept voluntarily and temporarily the conventions of the theatre and the illusion of reality onstage.

# Appendix
## Improvisation Exercises by Devotional

Here is a list of improvisation exercises designed to complement each devotional. Although these exercises are a lot of fun, please do not feel that they must be used in connection with the corresponding devotionals. You may use these exercises (some of which may already be familiar to you) as you see fit. They certainly are not intended to invoke profound discussion. Instead, they are fun rehearsal tools for actors—tools that bear only a subtle application to the devotional themes associated with them.

One note about the *get-fors*. Each of the *get-fors* mentioned in the exercises is a suggestion that players get from one another or from an audience (if there is one). In other words, players *get* a specific suggestion *for* the scene they are about to play.

"Take chances, make mistakes, get messy!"

—Mrs. Frizzle, *The Magic School Bus*

### Devotional: "What's My Motivation?"

Exercise: "GO!"

Players form a circle, facing in, shoulder to shoulder. One player (Player 1) points to another player (Player 2). Player 2 says "Go!" to Player 1. As soon as the command is shouted, Player 1 takes Player 2's place in the circle. As Player 2 moves, he or she immediately points at another player (Player 3) in the circle, and the process begins again.

This simple warm-up game requires players to concentrate on giving permission (saying "go!") *before* asking for permission (pointing). Speaking and pointing are not to be done at the same time by the same player in this exercise. What causes players to move from one location to the next, *really?* In other words, what's their motivation?

### Devotional: Fast-Food Drama Ministry

Exercise: "Half-Life"

A basic narrative improv for three players. *Get-fors:* a place and an occupation. Player 1 begins the story with specific pantomimed action that physically illustrates where we are (the place). After Player 1 has clearly introduced the environment or setting, Player 2 enters with a character relationship and begins dialogue with Player 1. After Players 1 and 2 have established the place and a relationship with one another, Player 3 enters the scene with a conflict or problem that interrupts the routine. The problem is resolved within a reasonable amount of time and the improvisational scene is over. Be sure that the occupation *get-for* is integrated into the scene as a key component.

Second half of the exercise: also, be sure to time the scene using a stopwatch. Do the scene again, exactly the same way, but in *half* the time of the first run. Do the scene a third time, exactly the same way, but in *half* the time of the second run. Continue repeating the unchanged scene, each time cutting the life of the scene in half from the previous run. Keep the half-life process going until you are down to three or four seconds! The last run is a scream!

When the scene is cut in half each time, what are the first things to be lost in terms of the integrity of the scene? How does the three-second scene compare with the first run of the scene? What could this imply in terms of our "hurriedness" and "corner-cutting" in our drama ministry efforts?

## Devotional: Prima Donna 101

Exercise: "Unlikely Place to Fall in Love"

A basic narrative improv with three players as described in "Half-Life" above. *Get-for:* an unlikely place to fall in love. The first time through the scene, the narrative develops normally as an improvisation. The place must be the *get-for* agreed upon at the outset. The only requirement of the plot is that two of the characters created by the players must fall in love before the plot complication is resolved.

After the first run of the scene is over, the same scene will be replayed three more times. In the first repeated scene, all of the characters become hyperactive. In the second repeated run they play the scene as a ballet (no talking!). The third run is played as monkeys (complete with sound effects). Each repeated run is hysterical, but be sure to solve the problem of playing the plot of the scene in the same order with (close to) the same dialogue every time.

As with most improvisation, this exercise requires a lot of give and take. Players must be willing to accept (rather than block) offers made by other players in order to keep the improv alive. Generally, no judgments should be made about the value of someone's suggestion or offer. Philosophically, there are no unworthy offers in improvisation, and improvisational problems cannot be solved when we always go for the gag or for the laugh. The bottom line of improvisation: make the other players look better than you. If *that* mantra doesn't begin to cure us of prima donna-itis, woe are we!

## Devotional: You Don't Bring Me Backdrops Anymore

Exercise: "Vacation Slide Show"

Two players sit and do the talking. Four other players stand and do the pantomiming. *Get-fors:* a popular vacation spot and a relationship. The two players who sit on either side of the playing space assume the roles represented in the relationship *get-for.* They are going to share with the audience a slide show from their most recent vacation (the other *get-for*) and to tell us about each slide.

Each slide in the show is created instantly by the four players by forming frozen vignettes or tableaux. It is important that the four players remain frozen with each slide, that they move into arbitrary but interesting poses every time, and that they are in their new pose before the sitting players describe the new picture. The job of the sitting players is to stay in their character relationships and to explain away everything we see in each slide. Sample framing language: "Let's take a look at our next slide" and, to wrap up, "On our return flight home here, Mom was …").

It's amazing how easily stories can be shared simply through the power of suggestion!

## Devotional: . . . And Gestus for All

Exercise: "Job Interview"

An exercise for everyone on the team to play together with as many players as desired. *Get-for:* an occupation. One player begins the exercise by assuming the role of a job interviewer for a particular position (the occupation *get-for*). The interviewer sits next to an empty chair awaiting the arrival of the first job applicant. The next player to come into the scene is the first applicant. The applicant has some kind of unusual, visible tic or quirk (examples: he floats, she speaks only in action movie quotes, he thinks someone is following him, she is ravenously hungry). The quirk must be sustained (floating, for instance) or be repeatable (movie quotes).

As the job interview proceeds, the interviewer gradually takes on the same quirk as the applicant, until they are both in full form together. Once the interviewer has made the complete transformation into the quirk, he or she creates a reason to leave the scene (examples: "I'll just go get an application for you" or "Let me go get my manager. I think he'd like to meet you"). Upon the interviewer's exit, the applicant changes seats (still with the quirk) and becomes the interviewer. A new player enters as a new applicant with a new quirk. The process begins all over again.

Every physical manifestation of a quirk in this exercise may be considered a form of Brechtian gestus. What a terrific way to practice the creation and identification of the gestus for other scene work to come!

## Devotional: "All of You Wonderful People in the Dark"

Exercise: "Freeze"

This familiar exercise is for all players and for all "audience" members.

*Get-for:* your choice (examples: a type of sandwich, something you might buy your grandmother, things associated with sports, an unusual reason to live, etc.). Two players begin the scene with the integrated *get-for.*

As the scene progresses, the positioning of the two players may suggest an entirely different scenario or situation to another player or audience member. Once this happens, the new player yells "Freeze!" and tags one of the current players. The new player replaces the tagged player in the same frozen position and immediately begins the new situation and character. The other original player follows suit and joins in with an appropriate character in the new situation. The process then begins all over again.

This exercise encourages total participation from player and audience alike in a shared activity. Both groups construct new meaning together in a collaborative way.

## Devotional: I Second That Emotion

Exercise: "Emotion Replay"

A basic narrative improv with three players as described in "Half-Life" above.

*Get-fors:* three different emotions (put the slowest or most inactive emotion in the middle and leave the most active/most interesting emotion for very last) and something you'd hear at a circus. The first time through the scene, the narrative develops normally as an improvisation. The circus *get-for* is integrated into the scene as well.

After the scene is over, it will be replayed exactly the same way three more times, but with all of the characters filled with the *get-for* emotions. In the first repeated scene, all of the characters will have the same first emotion. In the second repeated run they all have the second emotion. Same with the third run and third emotion. Each repeated run is hysterical, but be sure to solve the problem of playing the plot of the scene in the same order every time.

How do these emotions affect the meaning of the story? "Attitude is the mind's paintbrush; it can color any situation" (anonymous).

## Devotional: Pardon Me, but Your Subtext Is Showing

Exercise: "Contentless Scene"

This exercise comes by way of Robert Cohen's *Acting One* text and is for two players. Memorize the simple dialogue below.

A: Hey.
B: Hello.
A: What time is it?
B: Does it matter?
A: No, I guess not.
B: Almost noon.
A: What?
B: I said it's almost noon!
A: OK. Anything wrong?
B: What do you think?
A: Sorry to bother you.
B: No, no, it's all right.

Now put this memorized dialogue into a situation (example: a guy and a girl on a blind date). Try several relational situations of your own choosing. How does the subtext manifest itself in the situations and how does it significantly change from situation to situation? Is meaning or interpretation affected by these changes?

## Devotional: Send in the . . . Clones?

Exercise: "What Are You Doing?"

A familiar exercise for two players or multiple teams of two players each.

Player 1 asks Player 2, "What are you doing?" Player 2 responds with a specific activity (examples: "Painting with watercolors!" or "Changing a flat tire!"). As soon as Player 2 offers this response, Player 1 begins to pantomime that actual activity suggested by Player 2. Player 2 then asks Player 1, "What are you doing?" Player 1 responds with a suggested activity (while still doing the first activity) at which point Player 2 starts doing the second suggested activity. The process continues back and forth for several minutes. Speed and spontaneity are critical in this exercise. The goal is to avoid repeating activities or naming activities even remotely related to previous suggestions. It's tough!

Can we be original without thwarting our teammate? Also, consider Viola Spolin's famous "mirror" exercise with two players.

## Devotional: The Grand Illusion

Exercise: "Returns"

A classic endowment exercise in that it "endows" players with information by gradually implying clues, rather than directly stating facts. *Get-fors:* the name of a department store and three returnable objects of varying sizes and types. The exercise is good for three players who must leave the room and for one more experienced player who assumes the role of a store clerk at the returns counter.

Once a store name has been decided and the three players have left the room, the player/clerk will solicit *get-for* items from the audience for the three outside players to return one by one. The catch: the three outside players have no idea what they are returning; they only know that they are returning something. Their job is to figure out what they are returning based on the clues from the store clerk. The clerk's job is to use language that is purposely vague in order to give the clues, but to gradually provide more specific clues as the scene presses on. Eventually, the customer must state within the context of the scene what it is exactly he or she is returning.

"Returns" playfully demonstrates the results of human opacity (the opposite of transparency) on a very rudimentary level. Although the exercise has nothing to do directly with the spiritual dimensions of self-disclosure, it may serve as a light-hearted introductory tool to lead into further discussion regarding the nature of our human reluctance/resistance to reveal ourselves to God.

## Devotional: Go Ahead, Make My Deus Ex Machina

Exercise: "Gods of Mount Olympus"

A basic narrative improv with three players as described in "Half-Life" above along with three additional players who play the roles of Olympian gods from Greek mythology. *Get-fors:* an unusual object and a well-known holiday. Each of the *get-fors* should be integrated into the scene, and each of the "gods" (who remain off to one side) should be assigned to one of the players in the scene.

While the basic narrative improv proceeds as in the first part of "Half-Life," the Olympian gods "cause" things to happen to their particular players/characters in the scene. Examples: "The salesman has a fear of heights!" or "The customer can speak only in consonants!" or "The escaped convict has an uncontrollable obsession with broccoli!" In the course of the scene, the gods may choose three to four things to "happen" unexpectedly to their respective players until the problem in the scene is resolved.

Talk about divine intervention! This exercise makes contrived plots look like masterpieces! Hopefully, we don't have too many days like these.

## Devotional: "What's Past Is Prologue"

Exercise: "Narrative Flashback"

Another basic narrative improv with three players as described in "Half-Life" above. *Get-fors:* a celebrity and a favorite Christmas toy from childhood. During the scene (your choice as to when), each of the characters will have a "solo moment" in which he or she shares a brief memory flashback with the audience.

As they describe this moment from their past, the other two players immediately become slow-motion characters from the solo speaker's flashback. As soon as the flashback is over, the original scene resumes. The scene continues until all three characters have indulged in a flashback and as soon as they have also solved the conflict of the scene. Remember to include your *get-fors* in the scene!

Flashbacks are not nearly as helpful as prayer journals or rehearsal diaries for jogging memories and reminding us of where we've been so that we might remember where we are called to go in the name of Christ. Stay the course!